About the Game

The *Daily Detective* is a research game that can be used with your class, a group of classes, or the whole school. Each day, students are given a new clue, beginning with the most general and difficult. As the week progresses, the clues become more specific. Using a map, atlas, almanac, encyclopedia, or other tool, students research the clues. The object of the game is to use the daily clues to discover the name of the *Mystery State*.

One of the best ways to introduce the *Daily Detective* series to your students is to actually work through one week of clues with them to discover the identity of the *Mystery State*. Key words in each clue should help determine the best research tools to use each day. Most of the *Mystery States* can be solved by using just two basic tools—an atlas and encyclopedias.

Displaying the Daily Detective

To display the *Daily Detective*, you may want to create a bulletin board in your room similar to the one below. Staple a new clue on the board each day. Each Monday, you should also display "Last Week's *Daily Detective* Answer." You may also choose to display a list of the students who were successful in solving the previous week's mystery.

Extras

- Provide a small box in your room where students may deposit their answers. Instruct the students to write on a slip of paper their name, the answer, the date, and the time of day that they solved the *Daily Detective* mystery. You may wish to award a prize to the first person with the correct answer.

- Give Super Sleuth Awards (page 48) to all those who successfully solved the *Daily Detective* mystery.

- On a school-wide basis, set up a *Daily Detective* bulletin board in the school library or hallway. Choose a *Daily Detective* winner for each grade level.

- If your school computer is equipped with an encyclopedia or atlas on CD-Rom, teach your students to use the features of this research tool.

Alaska

Oil is the most valuable mineral in this state.

Tuesday

This state has more volcanoes than any other state.

Wednesday

$7,200,000

Secretary of State William H. Seward bought this state from Russia for only $7,200,000.

MT. McKINLEY

Thursday

The highest peak in the United States is found in this state.

Friday

This is the state's flag.

Last Week's Daily Detective Answer

Alaska, the United State's largest state, is famous for its majestic mountains and unspoiled wilderness. Mount McKinley is the highest peak in the United States. This beautiful state, which is rich in fish, timber, and oil, was bought from Russia for only $7,200,000.

Arizona

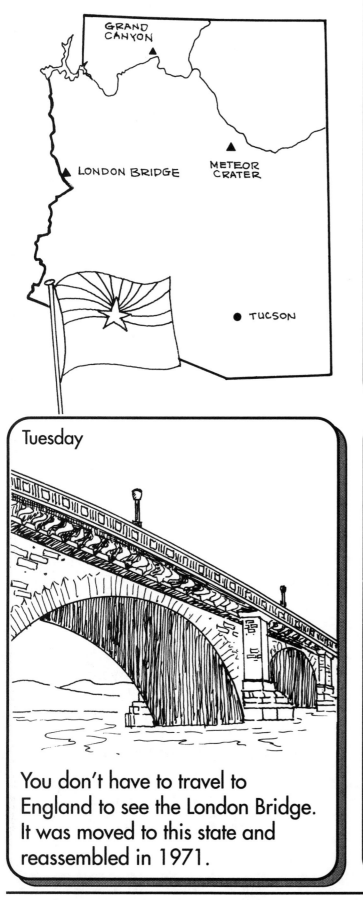

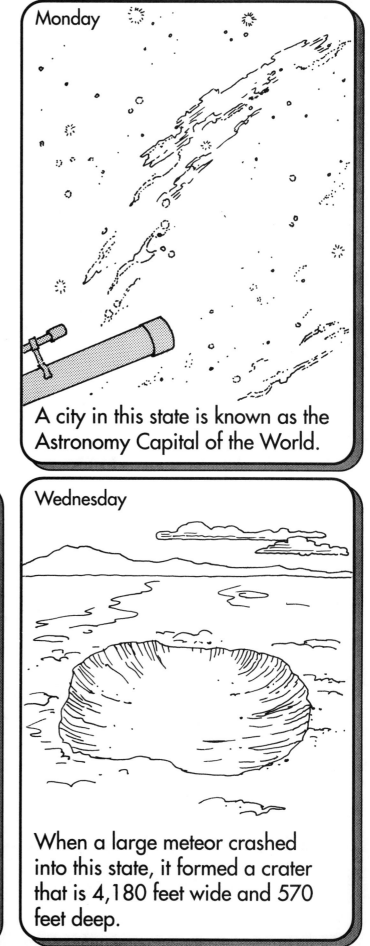

A city in this state is known as the Astronomy Capital of the World.

Tuesday

You don't have to travel to England to see the London Bridge. It was moved to this state and reassembled in 1971.

Wednesday

When a large meteor crashed into this state, it formed a crater that is 4,180 feet wide and 570 feet deep.

Thursday

Most of the people in this state live in desert areas.

Friday

This is the state's flower.

Last Week's Daily Detective Answer

Arizona is one of the fastest growing states. People are attracted to its pleasant winter climate and beautiful scenery. Many tourists visit Arizona to see the breathtaking Grand Canyon, the Painted Desert, and the Petrified Forest.

Arkansas

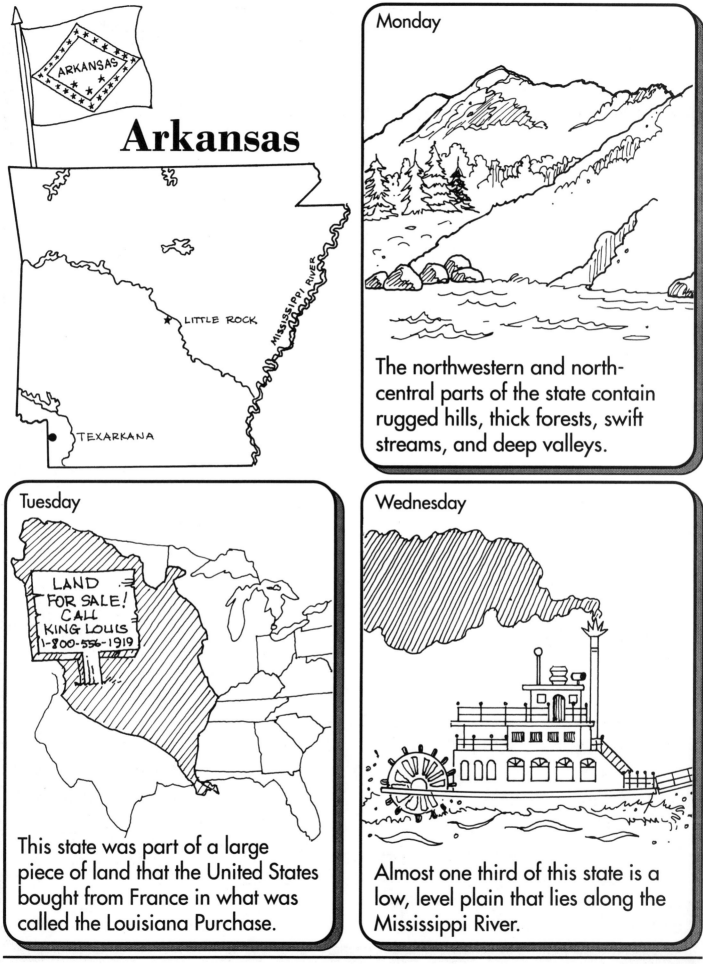

LITTLE ROCK

MISSISSIPPI RIVER

TEXARKANA

Monday

The northwestern and north-central parts of the state contain rugged hills, thick forests, swift streams, and deep valleys.

Tuesday

LAND FOR SALE! CALL KING LOUIS 1-800-556-1919

This state was part of a large piece of land that the United States bought from France in what was called the Louisiana Purchase.

Wednesday

Almost one third of this state is a low, level plain that lies along the Mississippi River.

Thursday

In 1932, a woman from this state, Hattie Caraway, became the first woman elected to the U.S. Senate.

Friday

TEXARKANA

STATE LINE

TEXAS

Half of the city of Texarkana is located in Texas and the other half is in this state.

Last Week's Daily Detective Answer

Millions of tourists travel to Arkansas each year to fish, swim, and boat in its beautiful lakes. The rugged forests and hills of the beautiful Ozark Mountain region are in the northern part of the state. Little Rock, the state's largest city, is also its capital.

California

Monday

Down, down, down! In this state you will find a desert with the lowest elevation of any place in North America.

Tuesday

The explorer John C. Frémont helped obtain this land for the United States.

Wednesday

This state has the tallest and oldest living trees in the world.

DEATH VALLEY

Thursday

The remains of saber-toothed tigers and other Ice Age animals have been found in this state's La Brea tar pits.

Friday

James W. Marshall discovered gold in this state while building a sawmill for John Sutter.

Last Week's Daily Detective Answer

California is known as the *Golden State*. Thousands of miners, known as "Forty-Niners", came here during the 1849 gold rush. Today, many people are attracted to California because of the warm, dry climate in the south and the beautiful scenery throughout the state. Others travel to California to visit Hollywood (the motion-picture capital of the world), Disneyland, and its many national parks and monuments.

Colorado

37°

0°

One of this state's borders is on the 37° north latitude line.

Tuesday

The Rocky Mountains cover less than one half of this state.

Wednesday

The Rio Grande River's source is in this state.

Thursday

The explorer Zebulon M. Pike discovered a spectacular 14,110 ft. mountain peak in this state.

Friday

This state is the home of the United States Air Force Academy.

Last Week's Daily Detective Answer

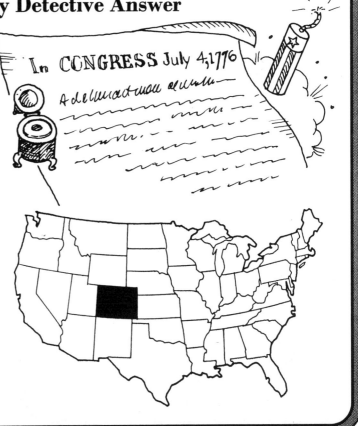

Colorado is called the *Centennial State*. It became a state in 1876, on the 100th anniversary of the signing of the Declaration of Independence. Colorado is known for its scenic Rocky Mountains. Though Pike's Peak is not Colorado's highest peak, it is its most famous mountain. Tourists frequent the state in the winter for the spectacular skiing it offers and in the summer for mountain climbing, white-water rafting, and camping.

Delaware

Monday

This state is located on a peninsula.

Tuesday

WOW!

That's a perfect arc!

This is the only state where part of its boundary is the arc of a perfect circle.

Wednesday

Oceangoing ships pass by this state when they travel to Philadelphia.

Thursday

Articles of Confederation

The Virginia Plan

...ersey Plan

NUMBER 1

We the people

On December 7, 1787, this was the first colony to become a state.

Friday

Cluck, cluck. This state bird is a chicken.

Last Week's Daily Detective Answer

DECEMBER 7, 1787

Delaware is called the *First State* because it was the first state to approve the United States Constitution. It is the second smallest state and shares a peninsula with parts of Maryland and Virginia. Wilmington, Delaware's largest city, has been called the *Chemical Capital of the World.*

Florida

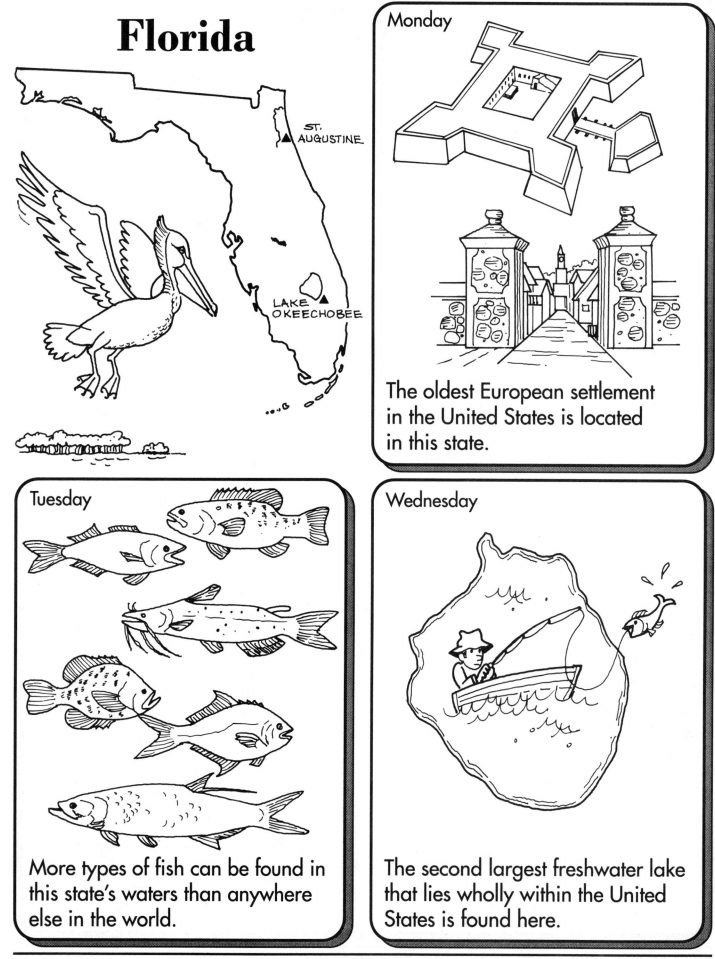

ST. AUGUSTINE

LAKE OKEECHOBEE

Monday

The oldest European settlement in the United States is located in this state.

Tuesday

More types of fish can be found in this state's waters than anywhere else in the world.

Wednesday

The second largest freshwater lake that lies wholly within the United States is found here.

Thursday

In 1513, the Spanish explorer Ponce de León became the first European to set foot in this state.

Friday

Oranges are this state's most important farm product.

Last Week's Daily Detective Answer

Florida is nicknamed the *Sunshine State.* Ponce de León was searching for the legendary Fountain of Youth when he discovered and then claimed Florida for Spain. Florida's warm, sunny climate and many beaches make it an ideal place for vacationers. Florida produces four-fifths of the nation's oranges and frozen orange juice.

Georgia

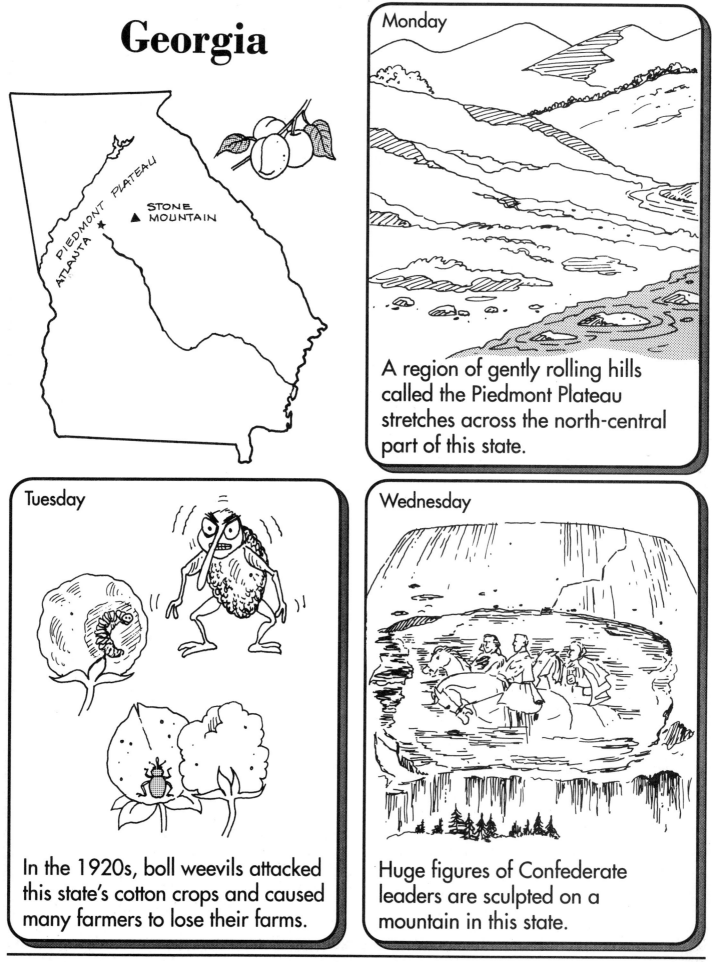

PIEDMONT PLATEAU

ATLANTA ★

▲ STONE MOUNTAIN

Monday

A region of gently rolling hills called the Piedmont Plateau stretches across the north-central part of this state.

Tuesday

In the 1920s, boll weevils attacked this state's cotton crops and caused many farmers to lose their farms.

Wednesday

Huge figures of Confederate leaders are sculpted on a mountain in this state.

Thursday

During the Civil War, General Sherman made his famous march across this state to the sea.

Friday

This state leads the United States in the production of peanuts, or *goobers*.

Last Week's Daily Detective Answer

Georgia is the largest state east of the Mississippi River. The mountains and ridges of the Appalachian Mountains form Georgia's northern border. Atlanta is Georgia's largest city, its capital, and an important center for trade and industry. Georgia is known as the *Goober State* because of its most important cash crop, peanuts. Jimmy Carter, the 39th President, is its best-known peanut farmer.

Hawaii

Kauai

Niihau

Oahu

ARIZONA

Molokai

Lanai

Maui

Kahoolawe

Hawaii

ACTIVE VOLCANO

Monday

In 1778, Captain James Cook became the first European to visit this state.

Tuesday

This state is the home of two active volcanoes.

Wednesday

In 1795, King Kamehameha I became ruler of most of this state.

Thursday

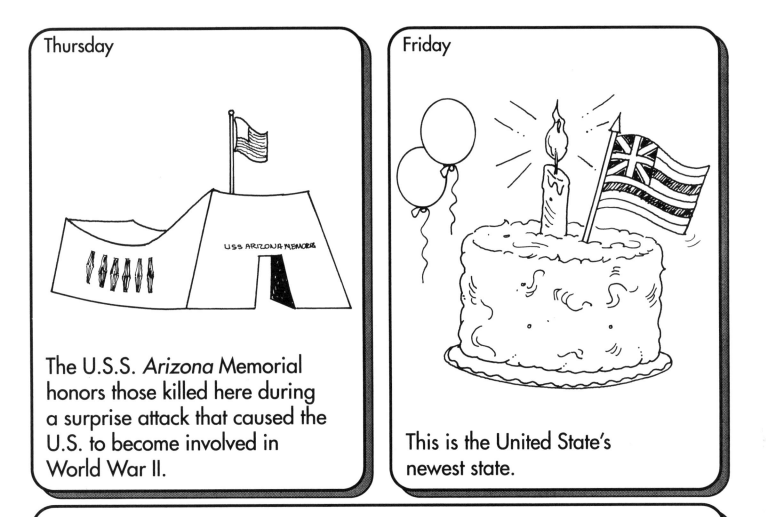

The U.S.S. *Arizona* Memorial honors those killed here during a surprise attack that caused the U.S. to become involved in World War II.

Friday

This is the United State's newest state.

Last Week's Daily Detective Answer

Hawaii, the *Aloha State*, is a chain of 132 islands formed by volcanoes in the Pacific Ocean. Hawaii's mild climate and beautiful scenery make it a popular place for vacationers. Many tourists attend a traditional Hawaiian *luau*, where typical island foods are served and entertainment usually includes the *hula*, a graceful Hawaiian dance. Sugar cane and pineapples are Hawaii's two main crops.

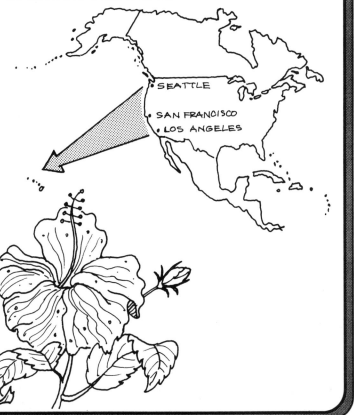

SEATTLE

SAN FRANCISCO

LOS ANGELES

Idaho

SNAKE RIVER

Monday

This state's international boundary is formed by the 49° north latitude line.

49°

0°

Tuesday

There are hundreds of waterfalls and caves in this state.

Wednesday

The majority of this state is covered by the Rocky Mountains.

Thursday

If you like French fries, you'll like this state. It grows more potatoes than any other state.

Friday

SNAKES

One-third of this state's western border is formed by the Snake River.

Last Week's Daily Detective Answer

Idaho is a Rocky Mountain state. It has some of the most rugged and beautiful areas in the United States. Some spectacular sights include Hells Canyon, the deepest canyon in the U.S., and the Shoshone Falls which are higher than Niagara Falls. Visitors come to Idaho to hunt, fish, ski, and take exciting boat trips down its swift rivers. Idaho grows more potatoes than any other state.

Illinois

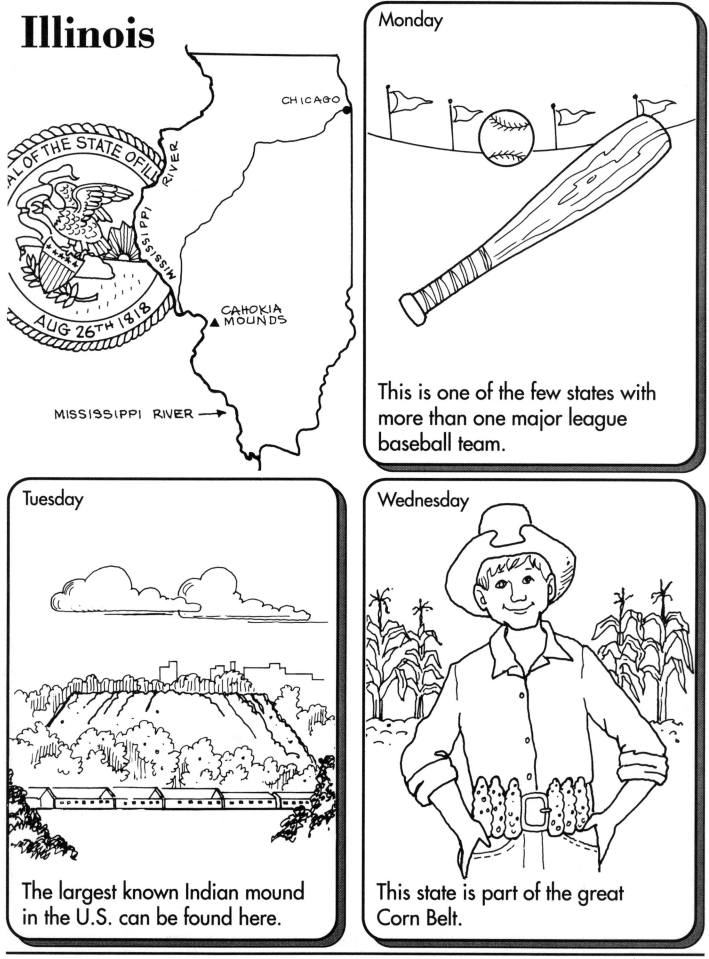

CHICAGO

MISSISSIPPI RIVER

CAHOKIA MOUNDS

AUG 26TH 1818

MISSISSIPPI RIVER →

Monday

This is one of the few states with more than one major league baseball team.

Tuesday

The largest known Indian mound in the U.S. can be found here.

Wednesday

This state is part of the great Corn Belt.

Thursday

This state is bordered by "Old Man River" and one of the Great Lakes.

Friday

This state is nicknamed the *Land of Lincoln* because Abraham Lincoln lived most of his life here.

Last Week's Daily Detective Answer

Illinois is more populated than any other Midwestern state. Chicago, the largest city in Illinois, is one of the world's leading industry and transportation centers. However, most of Illinois is covered with rich farmland. Corn and soybeans are its two most valuable crops.

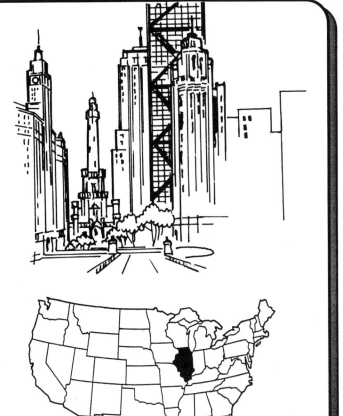

Kentucky

CHURCHILL DOWNS

FORT KNOX

OHIO RIVER

Monday

One of North America's most important waterways forms this state's northern border.

Tuesday

This state is one of the leading coal-mining states.

Wednesday

Mr. President

The 16th President of the United States was born in this state.

Thursday

Gold! Gold! Gold! Most of the gold owned by the U.S. government is kept in Fort Knox.

Friday

If you love to watch horse races come to Churchill Downs located in this state.

Last Week's Daily Detective Answer

Kentucky is known as the *Blue Grass State.* Its borders touch two great U.S. land features—the Appalachian Mountains on the east and the Mississippi River on the west. Kentucky is famous for its thoroughbred race horses and the most famous horse race in the country—the Kentucky Derby. Many come to Kentucky to see the Mammoth Cave, its most famous natural wonder, and Cumberland Falls, sometimes called the *Niagara of the South.* It is also one of the leading states in producing tobacco and in mining coal.

Louisiana

Monday

This state is part of the large piece of land that the United States bought from France.

Tuesday

The French explorer la Salle named this area after his king.

Wednesday

This state is known as the *Bayou State* because of its many bayous.

Thursday

The Mississippi Delta covers about one-fourth of this state.

Friday

If you love jazz, come to Preservation Hall in this state and listen to some of the best.

Last Week's Daily Detective Answer

Louisiana lies where the Mississippi River meets the Gulf of Mexico. Ocean and river water routes have helped make Louisiana one of the U.S.'s busiest commercial areas. Millions of visitors come to Louisiana each year to visit its largest city, New Orleans. Tourists love to visit the French quarter to enjoy the delicious Cajun and Creole foods, to listen to New Orleans-style jazz, and to participate in the festivities of the Mardi Gras.

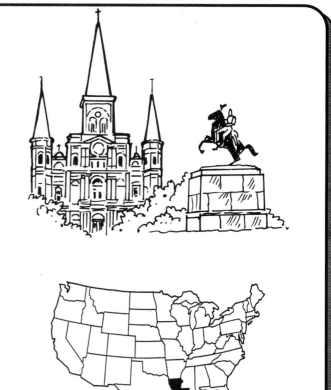

Maine

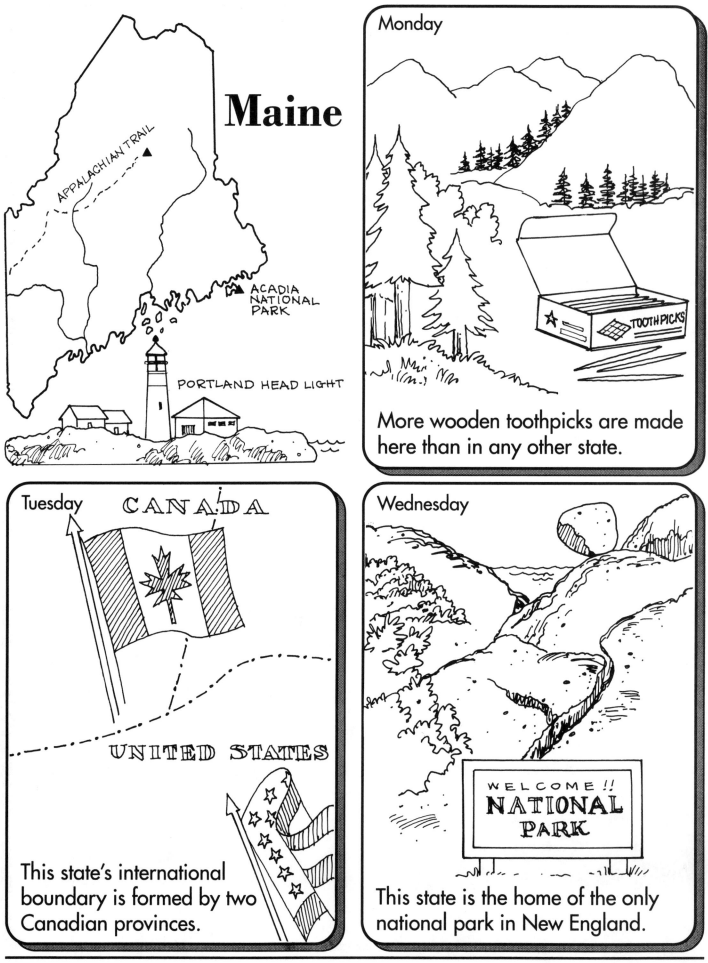

APPALACHIAN TRAIL

ACADIA NATIONAL PARK

PORTLAND HEAD LIGHT

Monday

More wooden toothpicks are made here than in any other state.

TOOTHPICKS

Tuesday

CANADA

UNITED STATES

This state's international boundary is formed by two Canadian provinces.

Wednesday

WELCOME !! NATIONAL PARK

This state is the home of the only national park in New England.

Thursday

One of the oldest lighthouses in America is in this state.

Friday

This is the easternmost state in the United States.

Last Week's Daily Detective Answer

Maine is the largest New England state. Ninety percent of it is covered by forests. The beautiful rocky coast and majestic mountains make it a summer vacationer's paradise. Maine is an important leader in wood processing and fishing. Nothing beats a delicious Maine lobster.

Massachusetts

Monday

ENGLAND

CHARTER
1629

Please let the
Puritans live
here.
Thank you.
King Charles I

In 1629 King Charles I of England gave the Puritans permission to settle in this state.

CONCORD • • LEXINGTON BOSTON

PLYMOUTH

NANTUCKET SOUND

Tuesday

Mr. President

Mr. President   Mr. President   Mr. President

Four United States Presidents were born in this state.

Wednesday

HISTORIC CITIES

This state contains many of the United State's most historic cities.

Thursday

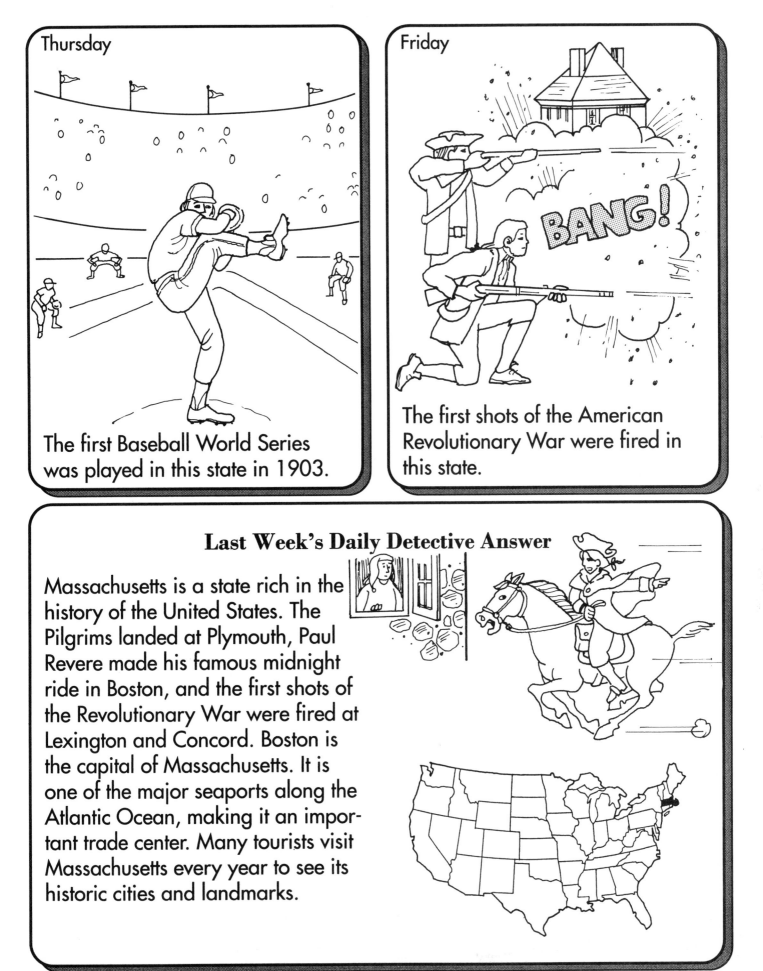

The first Baseball World Series was played in this state in 1903.

Friday

BANG!

The first shots of the American Revolutionary War were fired in this state.

Last Week's Daily Detective Answer

Massachusetts is a state rich in the history of the United States. The Pilgrims landed at Plymouth, Paul Revere made his famous midnight ride in Boston, and the first shots of the Revolutionary War were fired at Lexington and Concord. Boston is the capital of Massachusetts. It is one of the major seaports along the Atlantic Ocean, making it an important trade center. Many tourists visit Massachusetts every year to see its historic cities and landmarks.

Michigan

Lake Superior

MACKINAC ISLAND

Lake Huron

Lake Michigan

DETROIT

Lake Erie

Monday

This state's largest island is a beautiful wilderness national park.

Tuesday

STATE SHORELINE 3,288 mi.

This state's shoreline is 3,288 miles long. Only Alaska's is longer.

Wednesday

If you like cherry pie, come to this state. It has the largest production of cherries in North America.

Thursday

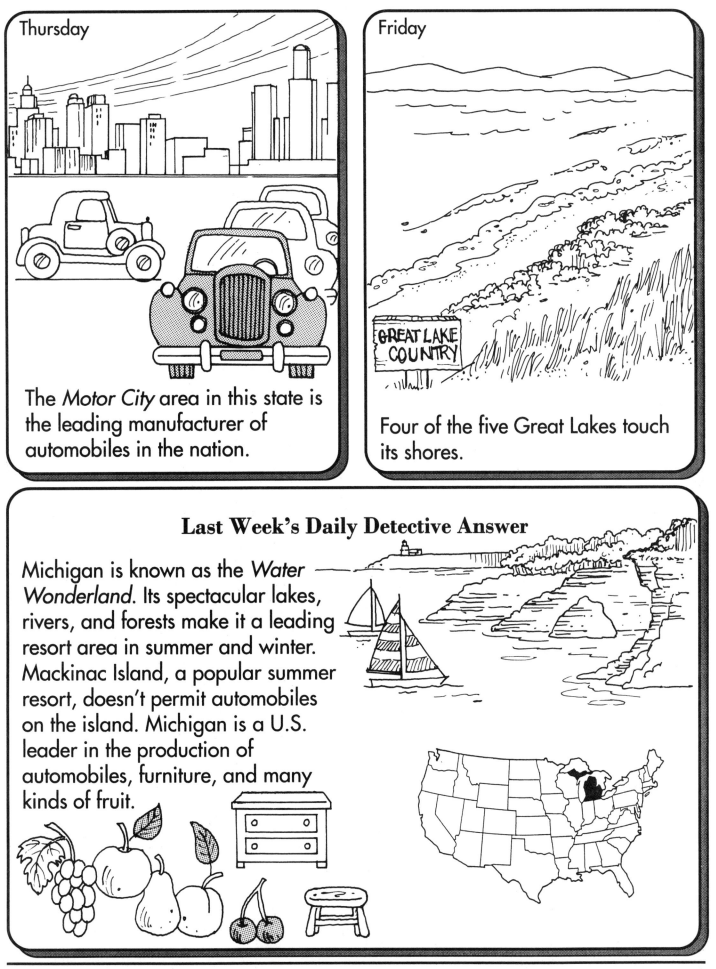

The *Motor City* area in this state is the leading manufacturer of automobiles in the nation.

Friday

GREAT LAKE COUNTRY

Four of the five Great Lakes touch its shores.

Last Week's Daily Detective Answer

Michigan is known as the *Water Wonderland*. Its spectacular lakes, rivers, and forests make it a leading resort area in summer and winter. Mackinac Island, a popular summer resort, doesn't permit automobiles on the island. Michigan is a U.S. leader in the production of automobiles, furniture, and many kinds of fruit.

Montana

▲ CUSTER'S LAST STAND

WHOA

COWBOYS HAVE THE RIGHT OF WAY

Monday

PACIFIC OCEAN

ATLANTIC OCEAN

The Continental Divide winds through this state. Rivers to the west of the Divide flow to the Pacific Ocean and those to the east of the Divide flow to the Atlantic Ocean.

Tuesday

YELLOWSTONE NATIONAL PARK ENTRANCE

Three of the five entrances to the oldest national park in the world are found in this state.

Wednesday

The Rocky Mountains cover the western two-fifths of this state.

Thursday

In 1916, Jeannette Rankin of this state became the first woman to serve in the United States Congress.

Friday

The Battle of the Little Bighorn, known as "Custer's Last Stand," took place in this state.

Last Week's Daily Detective Answer

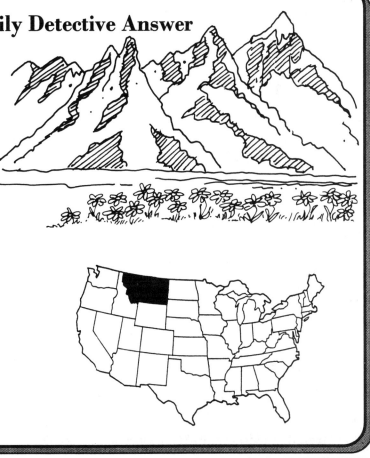

Montana, a land of snow-capped mountain peaks and large, open plains, is called *The Big Sky Country*. Each year outdoor enthusiasts come to Montana to hike, fish, ski, and travel through Glacier National Park. Tourists can experience Montana's Wild West heritage when they visit ghost towns, rodeos and Indian ceremonies. Montana's land is filled with rich deposits of copper, silver, and gold. On the open plains cattle graze and endless fields of golden wheat grow.

New York

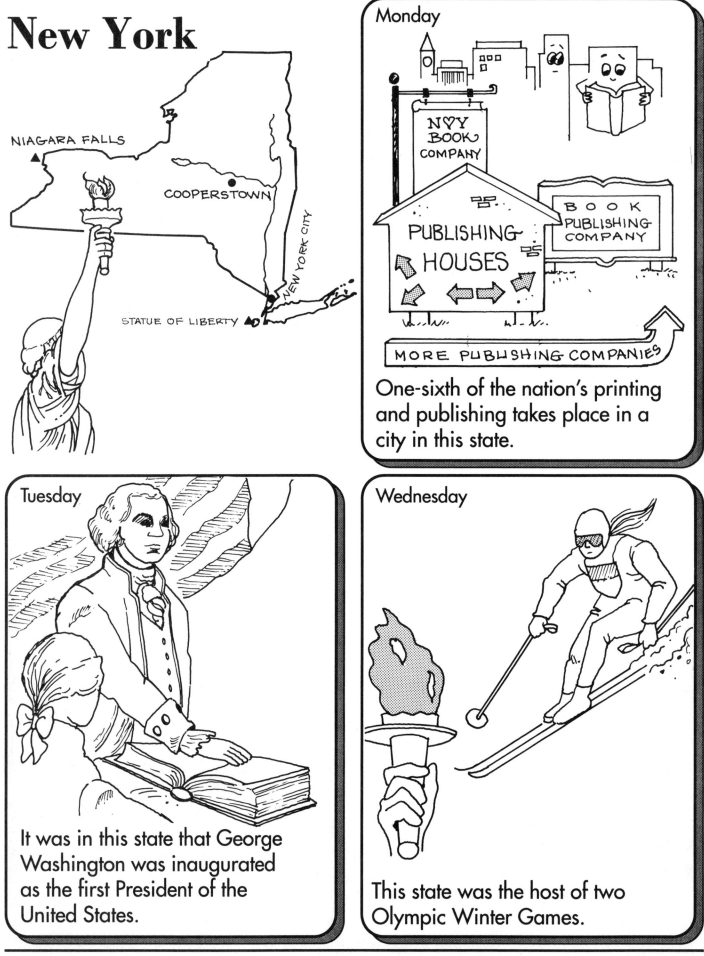

NIAGARA FALLS

COOPERSTOWN

NEW YORK CITY

STATUE OF LIBERTY

Monday

NY BOOK COMPANY

PUBLISHING HOUSES

BOOK PUBLISHING COMPANY

MORE PUBLISHING COMPANIES

One-sixth of the nation's printing and publishing takes place in a city in this state.

Tuesday

It was in this state that George Washington was inaugurated as the first President of the United States.

Wednesday

This state was the host of two Olympic Winter Games.

Thursday

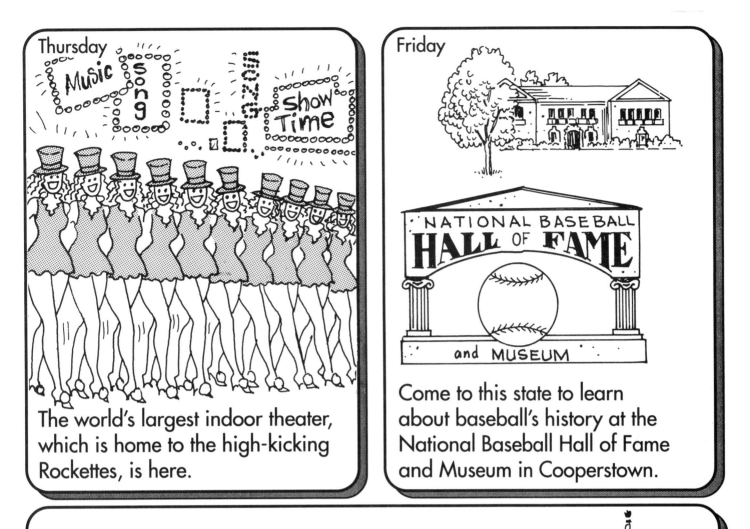

The world's largest indoor theater, which is home to the high-kicking Rockettes, is here.

Friday

Come to this state to learn about baseball's history at the National Baseball Hall of Fame and Museum in Cooperstown.

Last Week's Daily Detective Answer

New York, the *Empire State*, was one of the original 13 colonies. Today, New York outranks all states in banking and wholesale trade and ranks second in retail trade and manufacturing. New York City is the largest city in the United States and one of the largest in the world. The Statue of Liberty, Niagara Falls, the Empire State Building, and the Metropolitan Museum of Art are just a few of the many interesting places to visit in New York.

Ohio

CANTON

GREAT
SERPENT
MOUND

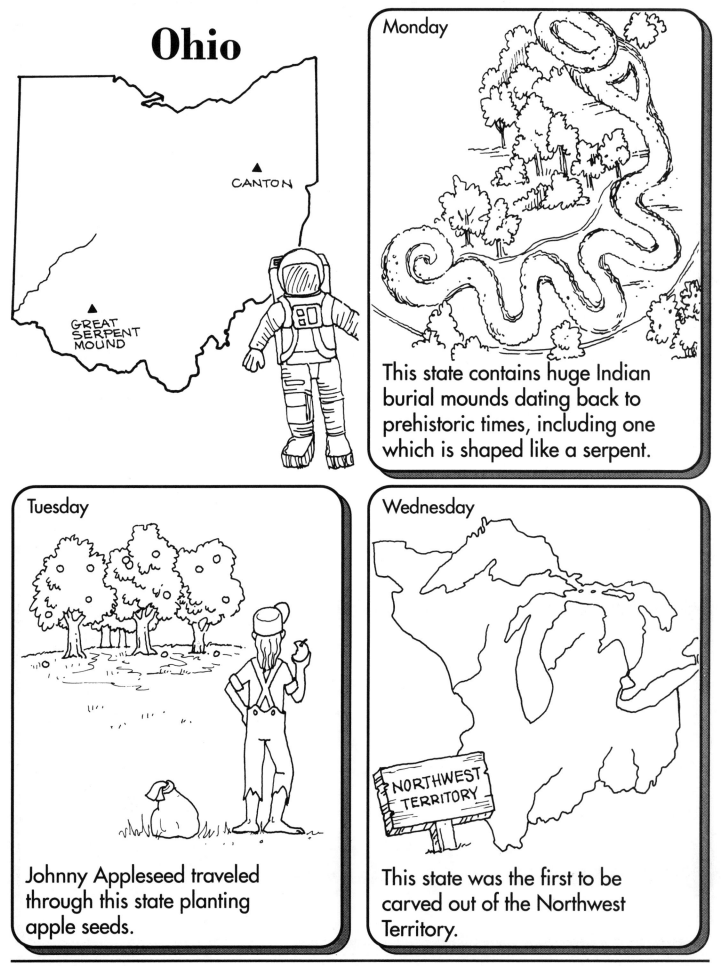

Monday

This state contains huge Indian burial mounds dating back to prehistoric times, including one which is shaped like a serpent.

Tuesday

Johnny Appleseed traveled through this state planting apple seeds.

Wednesday

NORTHWEST TERRITORY

This state was the first to be carved out of the Northwest Territory.

Thursday

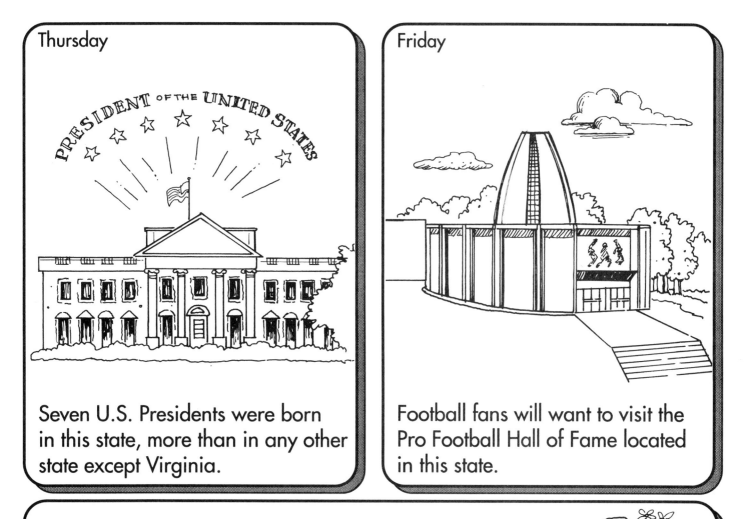

Seven U.S. Presidents were born in this state, more than in any other state except Virginia.

Friday

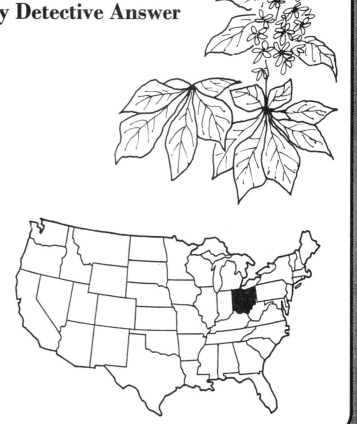

Football fans will want to visit the Pro Football Hall of Fame located in this state.

Last Week's Daily Detective Answer

Ohio, the *Buckeye State*, is one of the leading industrial states in the United States. It claims to be the birthplace of many famous people, including seven U.S. Presidents; two famous astronauts, John H. Glenn, Jr., and Neil A. Armstrong; and several inventors, including Thomas A. Edison and the Wright brothers. Columbus is the state's largest city and state capital.

Oregon

Monday

This state is the nation's leader in lumber production.

Tuesday

John's Furs

John Jacob Astor built a fur trading post in this state in 1811. It became the first white settlement in the state.

Wednesday

The deepest lake in the United States is found in this state. It lies in the crater of an extinct volcano.

(map labels: FUR TRADING POST, PORTLAND, SALEM, OREGON TRAIL, CRATER LAKE)

Thursday

The Cascade Mountains in this state contain some of the highest peaks in North America.

Friday

This state contains the end of the longest overland trail used by early settlers as they traveled west in the 1800s.

Last Week's Daily Detective Answer

Oregon leads the nation in lumber production. Forests cover almost half of the state. Millions of tourists come to Oregon each year to visit its rugged Pacific coastline, majestic mountains, and lush evergreen forests. Over half of Oregon's population lives in the Willamette Valley, where most of its large cities lie. Portland is its largest city and Salem is its capital.

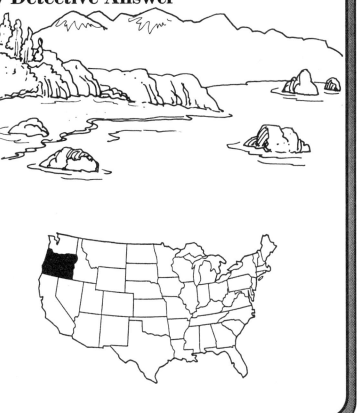

Pennsylvania

HERSHEY
PHILADELPHIA
YORK

Monday

STATELINE

This state shares its border with six other states.

Tuesday

All the anthracite (hard coal) produced in the United States is supplied by the eastern part of this state.

Wednesday

The capital of the United States was located in this state from 1790 to 1800.

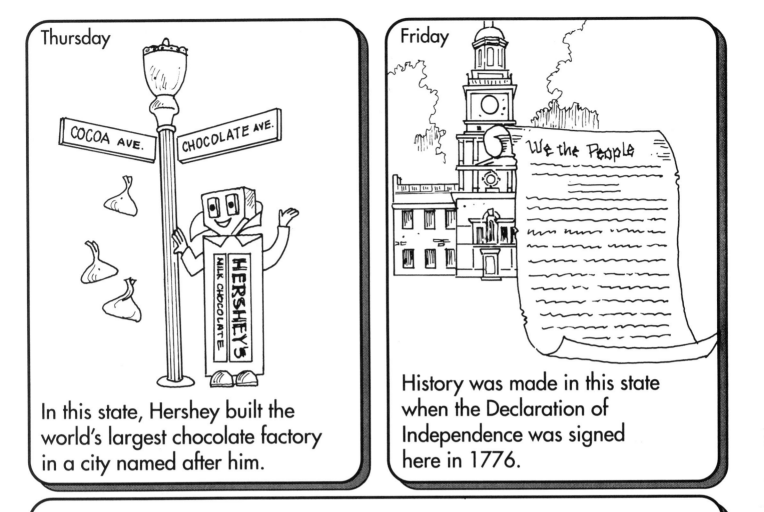

Thursday

In this state, Hershey built the world's largest chocolate factory in a city named after him.

Friday

History was made in this state when the Declaration of Independence was signed here in 1776.

Last Week's Daily Detective Answer

Pennsylvania is one of our nation's most historic states. King Charles II of England gave the land that is now Pennsylvania to a Quaker named William Penn. The word *Pennsylvania* means *Penn's Woods*. Philadelphia, known as the birthplace of the United States, is the home of the Liberty Bell and Independence Hall, where the Declaration of Independence was adopted. Today, Pennsylvania is a leading manufacturing and industrial center of the United States.

Texas

Monday

This state leads the nation in the raising of sheep.

Tuesday

HEY GUYS! The war ended last month!

The last battle of the Civil War was fought in this state at Palmito Hill on May 13, 1865. The soldiers had not heard that the war ended over a month before.

Wednesday

Chisholm Trail

Abilene

In the 1800s, cowboys drove longhorn cattle from this state along the Chisholm Trail northward to Abilene, Kansas.

Thursday

NASA built the Manned Spacecraft Center in this state.

Friday

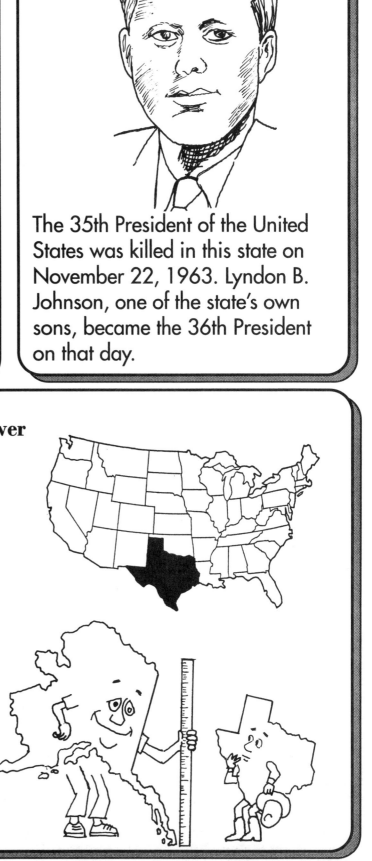

The 35th President of the United States was killed in this state on November 22, 1963. Lyndon B. Johnson, one of the state's own sons, became the 36th President on that day.

Last Week's Daily Detective Answer

Texas is known as the *Lone Star State* because of the single star on its flag. Only Alaska is larger in land area than Texas. The Alamo, a mission chapel that was the site of a famous battle in the Texas Revolution, still stands in what is now downtown San Antonio. Texas has more farmland than any other state and is a leading producer of cattle, sheep, and wool. It leads all other states in the production and refining of oil.

Wisconsin

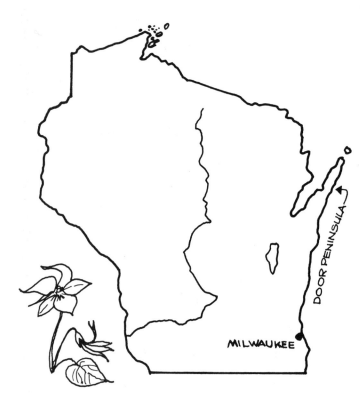

Jean Nicolet, the first explorer to arrive in this state, was disappointed to discover he had not landed in China.

Tuesday

Christopher L. Sholes, an inventor, journalist, and politician, helped invent the first practical typewriter in 1867 while working in this state.

Wednesday

This state is known as *America's Dairyland.* It leads the nation in the production of milk.

Thursday

This state's capital is named after the fourth President of the United States.

Friday

Thousands of people come to this state to visit the beaches, resorts, and countryside of Door Peninsula, located on the shoreline of Lake Michigan.

Last Week's Daily Detective Answer

Rich, green pastures and thousands of dairy herds have made Wisconsin a tremendous producer of milk and other dairy products. With its resource of thick forests, Wisconsin is one of the leaders in the production of paper products. Each year vacationers come to Wisconsin to swim, fish, and boat in its beautiful lakes, and hunt in its many forests. Milwaukee, Wisconsin's largest city, is located along the shores of Lake Michigan.

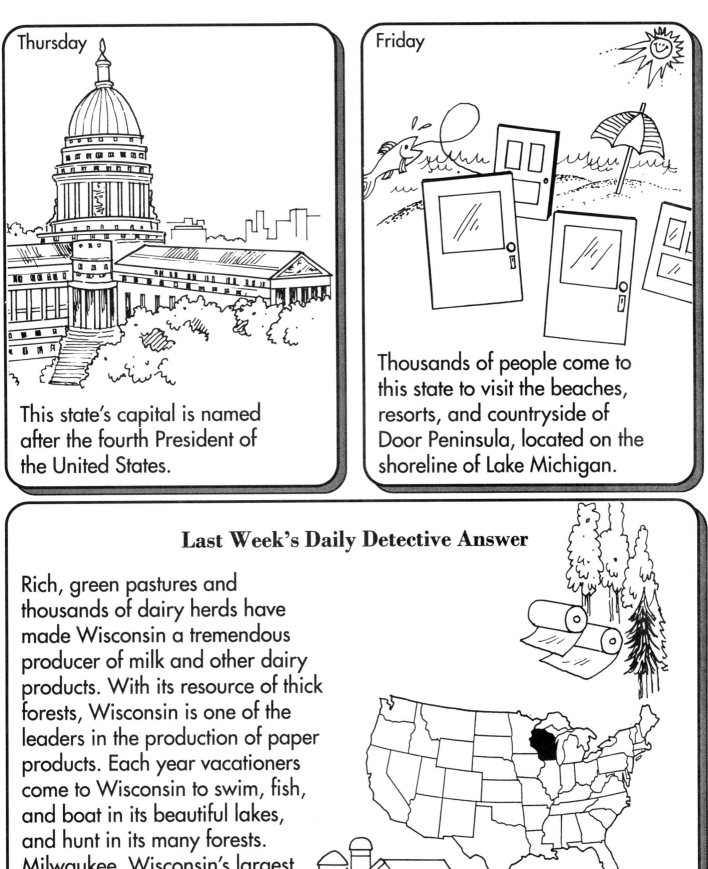

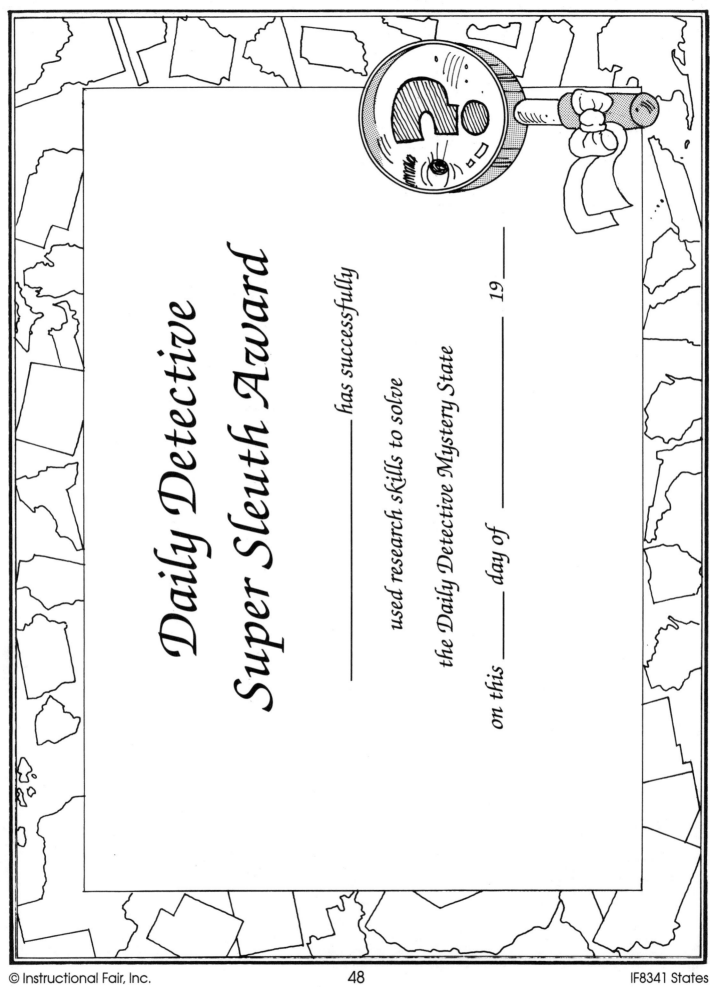

Daily Detective
Super Sleuth Award

_____ has successfully

used research skills to solve

the Daily Detective Mystery State

on this _____ day of _____ 19 _____